Money Riddles That That Count

Written by Margaret Fetty

STECK-VAUGHN
ELEMENTARY · SECONDARY · ADULT · LIBRARY

A Harcourt Classroom Education Company

www.steck-vaughn.com

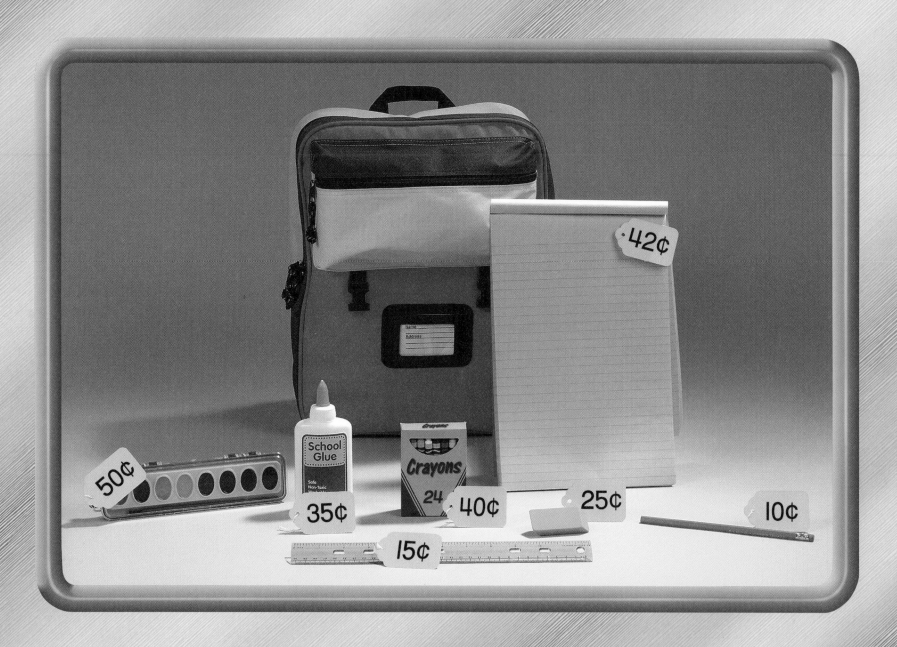

Read the money riddles in this book.

Count to see how much each school supply costs.

I am something that has two ends.

One end makes black marks go away.

The other end is a good *writer.*

Count how much I cost.

What am I?

a pencil   10¢

I am long and flat.

There are numbers on me.

I see how things **measure** up.

Count how much I cost.

What am I?

15¢   a ruler

I am made of rubber.

I make black marks go away.

I can rub answers the **wrong** way.

Count how much I cost.

What am I?

an eraser 25¢

You can buy me in a bottle.

I am white.

I make artwork **sticky** for you.

Count how much I cost.

What am I?

 9

glue

35¢

You buy us in a box.

You can use us to draw.

We add **color** to your pictures.

Count how much we cost.

What are we?

40¢ crayons

We have two sides.

We are flat and white.

We **line** up words.

Count how much we cost.

What are we?

paper   42¢

We come in many colors.

You mix water with us.

You use us to *brush* up on your artwork.

Count how much we cost.

What are we?

paints

50¢